EVERYDAY MYSTERIES

HOW DOES A THERMOMETER WORK?

By John O'Mara

Gareth Stevens
PUBLISHING

Please visit our website, www.garethstevens.com. For a free color catalog of all our high-quality books, call toll free 1-800-542-2595 or fax 1-877-542-2596.

Cataloging-in-Publication Data

Names: O'Mara, John.
Title: How does a thermometer work? / John O'Mara.
Description: New York : Gareth Stevens Publishing, 2021. | Series: everyday mysteries | Includes glossary and index.
Identifiers: ISBN 9781538256633 (pbk.) | ISBN 9781538256657 (library bound) | ISBN 9781538256640 (6 pack)
Subjects: LCSH: Thermometers–Juvenile literature. | Temperature measuring instruments–Juvenile literature. | Temperature measurements–Juvenile literature.
Classification: LCC QC271.4 O43 2021 | DDC 681'.2–dc23

Published in 2021 by
Gareth Stevens Publishing
111 East 14th Street, Suite 349
New York, NY 10003

Editor: Therese Shea

Photo credits: Cover, p. 1 Syda Productions/Shutterstock.com; pp. 3–24 (background) Natutik/Shutterstock.com; p. 5 Africa Studio/Shutterstock.com; p. 7 Towfiqu Photography/Moment/Getty Images; p. 9 bixstock/Shutterstock.com; p. 11 Jun Yong/EyeEm/Getty Images; p. 13 underworld/Shutterstock.co; p. 15 sirtravelalot/Shutterstock.com; p. 17 A. Ivashchenko/Shutterstock.com; p. 19 Sasiistock/Shutterstock.com; p. 21 Suppakij1017/Shutterstock.com.

Printed in the United States of America

CPSIA compliance information: Batch #CS20GS: For further information contact Gareth Stevens, New York, New York at 1-800-542-2595.

Find us on

CONTENTS

Boldface words appear in the glossary.

Useful Tools

Thermometers are important science tools! They measure temperature, or how hot or cold something is. They can measure air temperature, body temperature, and even the temperature of food. Have you ever wondered how different thermometers work?

Liquid-in-Glass Thermometer

One kind of thermometer has a liquid in a thin glass tube, or case. The tube has a part at the bottom called a bulb. Special liquids are used in these thermometers, such as the **metal** mercury.

bulb

When the air around the thermometer heats, the liquid's **volume** expands, or grows larger. This means that the **molecules** that make up the liquid move apart. The liquid takes up more space. It moves up the tube.

When the air cools, the liquid contracts, or its volume grows smaller. Its molecules grow closer together. The liquid moves down the tube. As the liquid in a thermometer expands and contracts, its highest point lines up with a mark. That's the temperature.

Temperature Types

Some thermometers measure different temperature **units**, such as Fahrenheit and Celsius. The United States often uses Fahrenheit for air temperature. Other countries use Celsius. These units are shown as °F (**degrees** Fahrenheit) or °C (degrees Celsius).

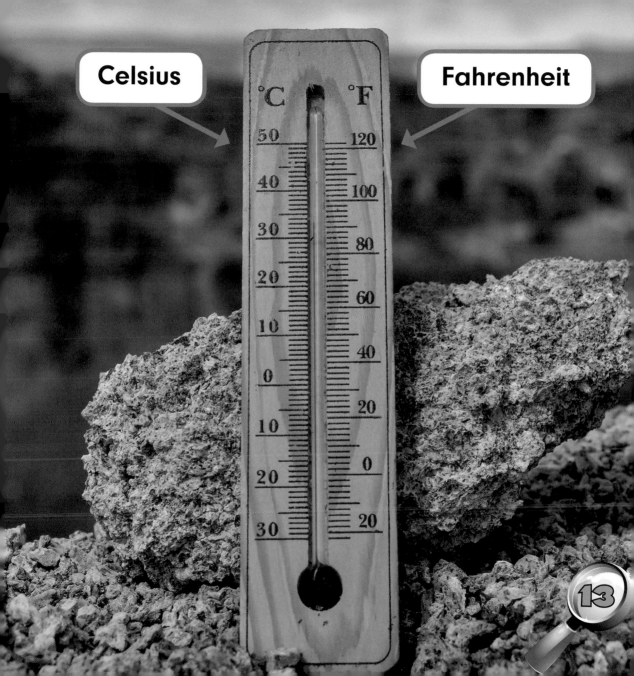

Fever Thermometers

A high or low body temperature can mean we're sick. We may use a different kind of thermometer to measure body temperature. We often put these thermometers in our mouths. Sometimes, they're called fever thermometers. Some give **digital** readings.

Infrared Thermometers

Infrared thermometers measure heat from a **distance**. They use a **lens** to gather infrared light from an object. In the thermometer, parts turn the light into heat and then into **electricity**. The amount of electricity is used to measure the temperature of the object.

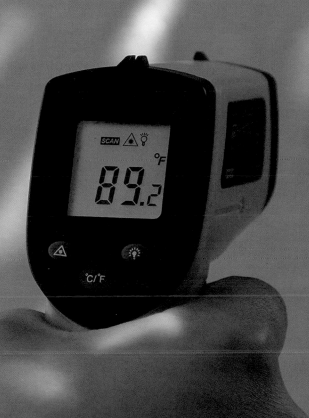

Powerful infrared thermometers were first used to measure the temperatures of objects in space, like stars! Then, scientists figured out they would be useful for people's health too. Infrared thermometers can measure body heat without even touching the body.

18

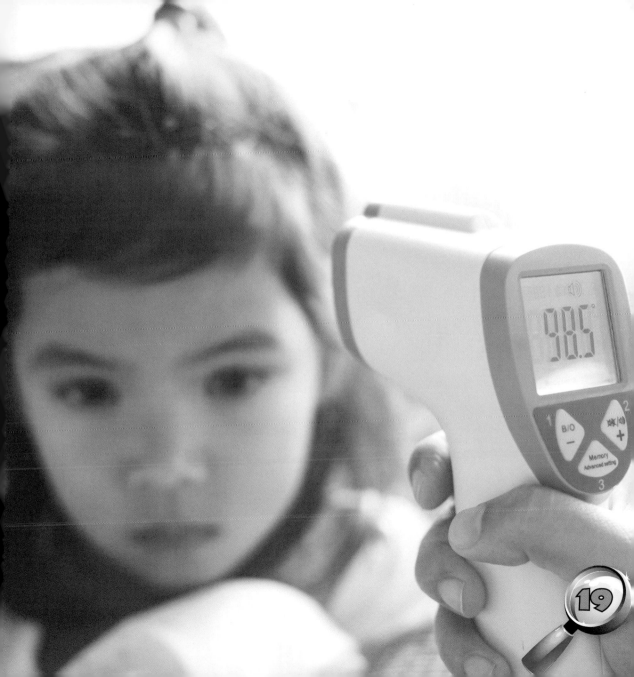

So Many Uses!

Different kinds of thermometers have been made for all kinds of uses. They're needed in doctors' offices, science labs, factories, homes, and many other places. Some people use thermometers every day. Think of all the thermometers you see each day!

HOW A MERCURY THERMOMETER WORKS

1 - The thermometer is a closed glass tube. It's partly filled with mercury.

2 - As the temperature around the thermometer's bulb changes, the mercury rises and falls as its volume expands and contracts.

3 - The highest point of the liquid is the temperature.

21

GLOSSARY

degree: a unit used for measuring temperature

digital: numbers on a screen that show information about something

distance: the amount of space between two things

electricity: a form of power carried through wires and used to operate machines

infrared: producing or using rays of light that people cannot see and that are longer than the rays that make red light

lens: a clear, curved piece of glass or plastic that changes the direction of light rays

metal: a shiny element found in the ground, such as mercury, iron, or copper

molecule: a very small piece of matter

unit: an amount of length, time, or temperature used for measuring

volume: the amount of space an object takes up

FOR MORE INFORMATION

BOOKS

Amstutz, Lisa J. *Thermometers*. North Mankato, MN: Pebble, 2019.

Schuetz, Kristin. *Temperature*. Minneapolis, MN: Bellwether Media, 2016.

Sherman, Jill. *Fire and Ice! Measuring Temperatures in the Lab*. New York, NY: PowerKids Press, 2020.

WEBSITES

How Thermometers Work
home.howstuffworks.com/therm.htm
Read more about what happens inside a thermometer.

Temperature
www.ducksters.com/science/physics/temperature.php
Learn interesting facts about temperatures.

INDEX